Ruthie's Easy Crocheted Scarves

by Ruthie Marks

Wrap yourself in creativity and get ready to make the most fun and sassy scarves ever. Whether elegant or funky, these easy patterns and great yarn colors will inspire you to get in step with fashion and make a truly unique statement. Patterns incorporate stripes, tubes, slits, and popcorn stitches for an exciting array of designs. The simplicity and intriguing versatility of Ruthie's creations will surprise you. Yarn choices run the gamut from mohair, chenille, and ribbon fibers to trendy eyelash and novelty textures. Add tassels, fringe, beads, or curly spiral tails for a fabulous finish, and you're ready to face the cold with panache.

Ruthie Marks teaches crochet at Little House, her local senior center in Ojai, California, where she learned the craft nine years ago. She has authored four crochet books and contributed her designs to numerous other books. She has also published patterns in more than a dozen newspapers and magazines. Garments, fashion accessories, and home décor items are her specialties. She and her husband, Roger, and their three cats live on ten acres outside of town. They produce their own electricity with the help of solar panels, and are building a sustainable home. Ruthie is a member of ACC, CGOA, SCD and TNNA.

contents

Basic Crochet Stitches and Techniques

yarn information

Scarves in this leaflet were made from various weights of yarn. Several different brands of yarn in the weight specified for each project may be used. It is best to refer to the yardage/meters when determining how many balls or skeins to purchase. Remember, to arrive at the finished size be sure to check your gauge.

making a chain

A chain starts with a slip knot (which does not count as a stitch). To make a chain, yarn over and pull through loop on hook.

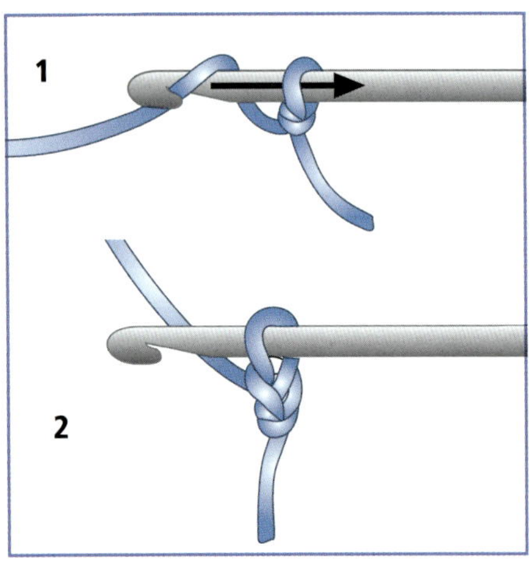

working in the chain

Method A: Insert hook under back loop of chain.
Method B: Insert hook under top two loops of chain.

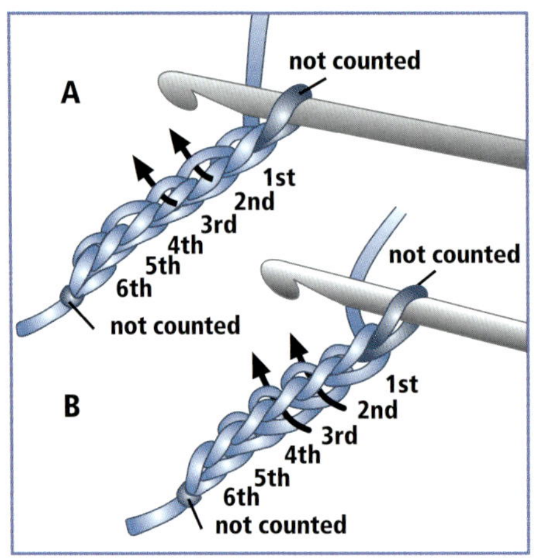

slip stitch

Insert hook, yarn over and pull loop through stitch and loop on hook.

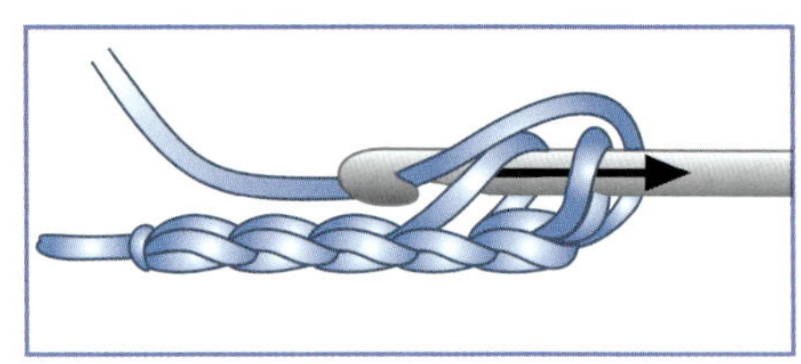

single crochet

Insert hook, yarn over and pull loop through, yarn over and pull through two loops on hook.

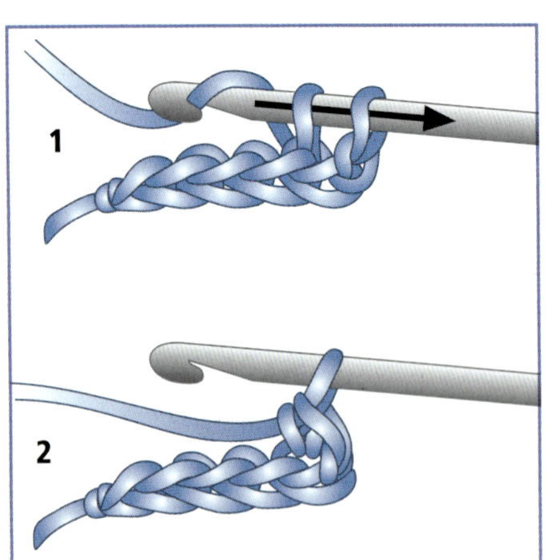

double crochet

Yarn over, insert hook, yarn over and pull loop through, yarn over and pull through two loops, yarn over and pull through remaining two loops.

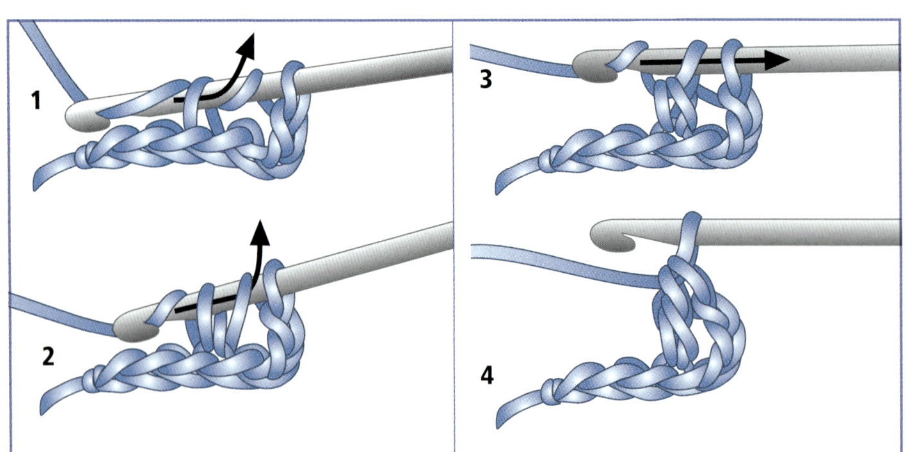

tassel

Cut a piece of cardboard a little longer than the length of tassel you want. Wrap the yarn around the cardboard the desired number of times. Slip a 9" piece of yarn under the yarn at top of cardboard and tie a knot tightly, leaving ends for later attachment to scarf. Cut yarn at other end. Tie another 6" piece of yarn around tassel about 1" to 1½" from top. Lay tassel on flat surface and trim ends evenly. Using tapestry needle, weave yarn ends at top of tassel into end of scarf and fasten securely. Weave all ends into center of tassel.

fringe

Cut a piece of cardboard a little longer than the length of fringe you want. Wrap the yarn around the cardboard the desired number of times and cut at one end. On RS of scarf, insert hook into edge st from back to front. Fold strands in half, hook folded ends around hook and pull through scarf; insert strand ends into lp pulled through and pull gently to tighten. (When yarn has been left at beg and / or end of rows to be incorporated into fringe, place these ends into lp pulled through by hook before pulling ends to tighten.) Trim ends evenly.

half double crochet

Yarn over, insert hook, yarn over and pull loop through, yarn over and pull through all three loops on hook.

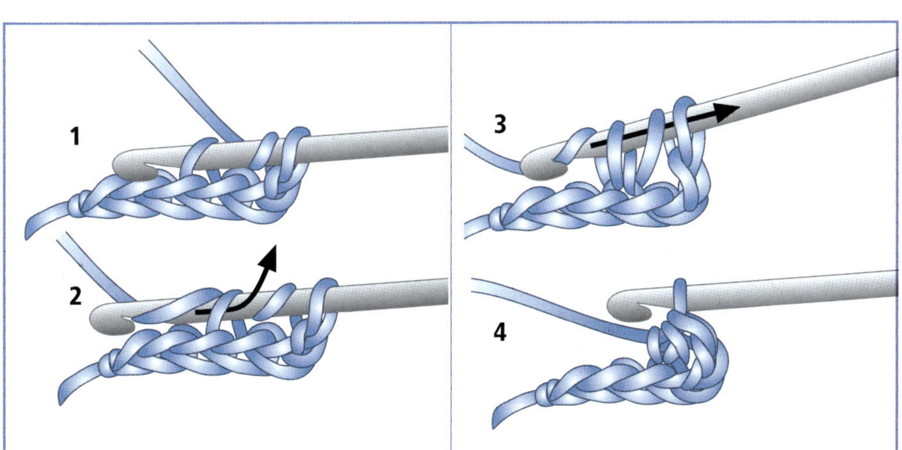

Abbreviations and Terminology

approx – approximately
beg – beginning
ch(s) – chain(s)
lp(s) – loop(s)
oz – ounces
rep – repeat
rnd(s) – round(s)
RS – right side
sp(s) – space(s)
st(s) – stitch(es)
tch – turning chain
tog – together
WS – wrong side
yds – yards
yo – yarn over (wrap yarn around hook)

Stitch Abbreviations (listed by height)

sl st – slip stitch
sc – single crochet
hdc – half double crochet
dc – double crochet
tr – triple (yo 2 times)
dtr – double treble (yo 3 times)
trtr – triple treble (yo 4 times)

Special Stitches

3(4)-dc bobble
6-dc popcorn
Bpdc – back post dc
Curlicue
Dc2(4)tog
Esc – extended sc
Fpdc – front post dc
Ldtr – linked double treble
Ltrtr – linked triple treble
Psc – picot single crochet
V-st – V-stitch

Slits, Slits, Slits One

Seven slits provide numerous options for wearing this scarf.

Finished size approx. 4" x 51"

materials

Sport weight yarn (250 yds./3.5 oz.), 1 skein green speckled (A)
Crochet thread (100 yds./1.6 oz.) 1 ball purple (B)
Size I/9 (5.5mm) and E/4 (3.5mm) crochet hooks
Tapestry needle

gauge

With I hook: 10 sts = 3"
9 rows = 4"

special stitch

Curlicue: (Sc, ch 11, sc in back bumps of second ch from hook and each ch to end [10 sc], sc) in same st.

instructions

Row 1 (WS): With A and I hook, ch 152, hdc in third ch from hook and in each ch across, turn — 150 sts.
Rows 2–4: Ch 2 (does not count as a st), *hdc in back lp only of first st, hdc in front lp only of next st, rep from * across, turn.
Row 5: Ch 1, sc in both lps of first 10 sts, *ch 10, skip 10 sts, sc in both lps of next 10 sts, rep from * across, turn.
Row 6: Ch 1, sc in each sc and into each ch st across, turn.
Rows 7–9: Rep rows 2–4, turn.
Row 10 (RS): Ch 1 (counts as sl st), sl st through both lps of each st across, Fasten off.

On other long side, with same side facing, attach with sl st and sl st in each st across. Fasten off.

BOTH ENDS

Row 1 (RS): With E hook, join B with sc, curlicue in next st, *sc in next 3 sts, curlicue in next st, rep from * to last st, sc in last st, turn — 15 sts evenly spaced across.
Row 2: Ch 1, sc in first st, *ch 1, skip curlicue, sc in next 3 sts, rep from * to last 2 sts, ch 1, skip curlicue, sc in last st, turn.
Row 3: Ch 1, sc in each st and ch-1 space across, turn.
Rows 4–6: Ch 1, sc in each st across, turn.
Rows 7–12: Rep rows 1–6, beg row 7 with ch 1, sc.
Rows 13–14: Rep rows 1–2, beg row 13 with ch 1, sc.
Row 15: Ch 1 (counts as first sl st), sl st in each st and ch-1 sp across. Fasten off.

Model made with Red Heart Wiggles (acrylic): #727 Green (A); J & P Coats Speed Cro-Sheen (cotton), #458 Purple (B).

Slits, Slits, Slits Two

With 8 slits there are multiple ways to wear this scarf.

Finished size approx. 4.75" x 53"

materials

Worsted weight yarn (120 yds./1.75 oz.), 1 skein each orange (A), yellow (B), blue (C)
Size G/7 (4.5mm) crochet hook
Tapestry needle

gauge

12 dc = 3"
2 rows dc = 1.25"

notes

On all rows using colors B and C (rows 3–13), leave an 8" tail at the beg and end of each row to be incorporated into the fringe. Turn at the end of each row.

instructions

Row 1 (WS): With A, ch 206, dc in fourth ch from hook and each ch across, turn — 204 sts.
Row 2: Ch 3 (counts as dc and first st), dc in each st across, ending last st in top of tch, drop A, pick up B, turn.
Row 3 (start leaving 8" tail): With B, ch 1, sc in each st across, ending last st in top of tch, drop B, pick up C, turn.
Row 4: With C, ch 1, sl st loosely in each st across, drop C, pick up B, turn.
Row 5: With B, ch 1, sc in top lp only of each sl st across, drop B, pick up C, turn.
Row 6: With C, ch 1, sc in first 12 sts, *ch 12, skip 12 sts, sc in next 12 sts, rep from * across, turn.
Row 7: Ch 1, sc in each st and into each ch across, turn.
Rows 8–9: Ch 1, sc in each st across, drop C, pick up B, turn.
Row 10: With B, rep row 6, turn.
Row 11: With B, rep row 7, drop B, pick up C, turn.
Row 12: With C, rep row 4, drop C, pick up B, turn.
Row 13: With B, rep row 5, drop B, pick up A, turn.
Rows 14–15: With A, ch 3, dc in each st across. Fasten off.

EDGING

Both Sides

With RS facing and A, join with sl st and sl st in each st across. Fasten off.

FRINGE

Work in all A ends. Use forty-eight 16" strands of B and C attached at ends of rows 3–13. Refer to instructions on page 3.

Model made with Bryson Kid-n-Ewe (wool/mohair): #680 Orange (A), #390 Yellow (B), #340 Blue (C).

Pretty, Pretty Pink

Eyelash yarn combines with crochet thread for a sassy look.

Finished size approx. 3" x 55"

materials

Cotton thread size 3 (150 yds./2.4 oz.) 1 skein rose (A)
Bulky weight (73 yds./.75 oz.), 2 skeins multicolor (B)
Size I/9 (5.5mm) crochet hook
Size G/6 (4.25mm) crochet hook
Tapestry needle

gauge

With I hook: 9 sts = 3"
6 rows = 3"

special stitches

Extended single crochet (Esc): Insert hook, yo and pull through, yo and pull through 1 lp (2 lps on hook), yo and pull through both lps.
V-stitch: Dc, ch 1, dc in same stitch.
4-dc bobble: Work 4 dc into st indicated until 1 lp of each remains on hook (5 lps on hook), yo and pull through all 5 lps.

notes

Center Portion: With I hook use one strand each of A and B.
End Portion: With G hook use one strand of A.

Model made with J & P Coats Royale Fashion, #775 Warm Rose (A); Trendsetter Shadow Eyelash (polyester), #1007 Passion Flower (B).

instructions

CENTER PORTION

Row 1: With I hook, ch 10, Esc in second ch from hook and each ch across, turn — 9 sts.
Row 2: Ch 1, Esc in each st across, turn.
Rep row 2 until 39" from beg, cut eyelash, turn.

FIRST END PORTION

Row 1 (WS): With G hook, 2 Esc in first st, *Esc in next 3 sts, 2 Esc in next st, rep from * to end, turn — 12 sts.
Rows 2–3: Ch 1, Esc in each st across, turn.
Row 4: Ch 3 (counts as dc and first st), V-st in next st, *skip next 2 sts, V-st in next st, rep from * to last st, dc in last st, turn.
Row 5: Ch 3, 4-dc bobble in first V-st, *ch 2, 4-dc bobble in next V-st, rep from * to last st, dc in top of tch, turn.
Row 6: Ch 1, sc in each st and 2 sc in each ch-2 space across, end last st in top of tch, turn.
Rows 7–18: Rep rows 4–6 four times, turn.
Row 19: Ch 1, sc in first st, 4-dc bobble in next st, *sc in next 2 sts, 4-dc bobble in next st, rep from * to last st, sc in last st. Fasten off.

SECOND END PORTION

With WS facing, rep rows 1–19 of First End Portion.

Reversible Delight

Blue on one side, green on the other — which color should I feature today?

Finished size approx. 7" x 58"

materials

Heavy worsted weight yarn (153 yds. / 1.75 oz.), 1 skein each green (A), blue (B)
Worsted weight yarn (164 yds. / 1.75 oz.) 1 skein multicolor (C)
Size N / 15 (10mm) crochet hook for scarf, K / 10.5 (6.5mm) for edging
Tapestry needle

gauge

5 sts = 3"
4 rows = 3"

special stitch

Extended single crochet (Esc): Insert hook, yo and pull through, yo and pull through 1 lp (2 lps on hook), yo and pull through both lps.

instructions

BODY

Make 2: 1 color A and 1 color B.
Row 1 (WS): With N hook and color A or B, ch 11. Esc in second ch from hook and in each ch across, turn — 10 sts.
Row 2: Ch 1, Esc in each st across, turn.
Rep row 2 until 58" from beg or to desired length. Fasten off.

EDGING

Place wrong sides of 2 pieces together. Using K hook and working through both layers, attach color C in any stitch with sl st. Working evenly around edges of scarf, (sl st, ch 3, sl st in first ch, ch 1) in each st. Fasten off.

Model made with Katia Ingenua (mohair / nylon / wool), #15 Green (A), #70440 Blue (B); Artful Yarns Portrait (mohair / viscose / polyester), #171 Girl Before a Mirror (C).

Mirror Image

Very tall stitches made with a variegated yarn are linked horizontally to produce an eye-catching effect.

Finished size approx. 5" x 65"

materials

Worsted weight yarn (348 yds./6 oz.), 1 skein multicolor
Size K/10.5 (6.5mm) crochet hook
Tapestry needle

gauge

11 Ltrtr = 4"
1 row Ltrtr = 1.75"

special stitches

Linked triple treble (Ltrtr): *Insert hook down through upper of 4 horizontal lps on post of last st made, yo and pull lp through, rep from * with 3 remaining horizontal lps (5 lps on hook), insert hook into next st, yo and pull lp through (6 lps on hook), (yo and pull through 2 lps) 5 times.
Ltrtr at beg of row: Ch 6 and treat second, third, fourth and fifth chs from hook as 4 horizontal lps.

instructions

SIDE 1

Row 1 (RS): Ch 170, sc in second ch from hook and each ch across, turn — 169 sts.
Row 2: Ch 1, sc in each st across, turn.
Row 3: Ch 6 (counts as trtr and first st), Ltrtr in each st across. Fasten off.

SIDE 2

(RS) Working in unused lp of foundation ch: Rep rows 1–3 of Side 1.

SHORT ENDS

Row 1 (RS): Join with sc and place 14 sc evenly across, turn — 14 sts.
Rows 2–5: Ch 1, sc in each st across, turn. Fasten off at the end of row 5.

Model made with Red Heart Super Saver (acrylic), #0968 Starbrights.

Long Stripes

Striped yarn with long intervals of color and a simple stitch make this easy scarf an eye-pleaser.

Finished size approx. 4" x 75" without fringe

materials

Worsted weight yarn (348 yds. / 6 oz.), 1 skein pastel multicolor

Size K / 10.5 (6.5mm) crochet hook

Tapestry needle

gauge

11 hdc = 4"

7 rows = 4"

note

Ch 2 at beginning of rows 2–7 does not count as first hdc.

instructions

Row 1: Ch 202, hdc in third ch from hook and each ch across, turn — 200 sts.

Rows 2–7: Ch 2, hdc in back lp only of each st across, turn.

Final row: Ch 1 and sl st around entire scarf, placing sts evenly along short edges, sl st to beg sl st, turn.

LOOPY FRINGE

First short end: Ch 1, sc in first st, *ch 20, sc in next st, rep from * across. Fasten off.

Second short end: With same side facing, join at one edge with sc, *ch 20, sc in next st, rep from * across. Fasten off.

Model made with Red Heart Super Saver (acrylic), #317 Reef Stripe.

Purple Passion

Surface embellishment and glass beads create an elegant pattern on a richly colored background.

Finished size approx. 3" x 52" without fringe

materials

Worsted weight yarn (190 yds. / 4 oz.), 1 skein burgundy (A)

Sport weight yarn (93 yds. / 1.75 oz.), 1 hank purple multicolor (B)

12 glass beads from local craft shop

Size K / 10.5 (6.5mm) and L / 11 (8mm) crochet hooks for scarf

Size E / 4 (3.5mm) crochet hook for embellishment

Tapestry needle

gauge

8 sc = 3"

7 rows = 3"

notes

Leave a 10" tail at beg and end of each row. Work in back lps only and do not turn work. When working with A, begin and end each row with 2 stitches using K hook. Use the L hook for the rest of each row.

instructions

With L hook and color A, ch 136.

Row 1 (RS): Change to K hook and sc in second ch from hook and next ch, change to L hook and sc across to last 2 ch, change to K hook and sc in last 2 ch. Fasten off — 135 sts.

Rows 2–7: With K hook attach yarn with a sc in first st, sc in next st, change to L hook and sc across to last 2 sts, change to K hook and sc in last 2 sts. Fasten off.

BOTH LONG EDGES

(RS) With L hook, attach with sl st to first st and each st across. Fasten off.

EMBELLISHMENTS

Work on rows 2, 4 and 6.

(RS) With E hook and B, (sl st, ch 3, sl st) in each free lp across. Fasten off. Work in ends.

FRINGE

Work in all ends except for 6 (one on each side of embellishment rows). Tie each pair of ends together in a fringe knot. Thread 1 bead onto each strand. Tie fringe knot below beads. There will be 3 fringes and 6 beads on each end.

Model made with Brown Sheep Lamb's Pride Worsted, (wool / mohair), M-25 Garnet (A); Classic Elite Imagine (cotton / rayon), #9203 Grape Arbor (B).

Lace And Spirals

*V-stitches, bobbles and perky spirals —
what a great combination!*

Finished size approx. 4" x 58" without spirals

materials

Worsted weight yarn (200 yds. / 3.5 oz.), 2 skeins green
Size H / 6 (4mm) crochet hook
Tapestry needle

gauge

15 sts = 4"
4-row repeat = 2"

special stitches

V-stitch: Dc, ch 1, dc in st indicated.
3-dc bobble: Work 3 dc into st indicated until 1 lp of each dc remains on hook (4 lps on hook), yo and pull through all 4 lps.

instructions

Row 1 (WS): Ch 16, sc in second ch from hook and each ch across, turn — 15 sts.
Row 2: Ch 1, sc in each st across, turn.
Row 3: Ch 3 (counts as dc and first st), V-st in next st, *skip 2 sts, V-st in next st, rep from * to last st, dc in last st, turn — 5 V-sts.
Row 4: Ch 3, 3-dc bobble in V-st, *ch 2, 3-dc bobble in next V-st, rep from * across, dc in tch, turn — 5 bobbles.
Row 5: Ch 1, sc in each st and 2 sc in each ch-2 sp across, ending sc in top of tch, turn — 15 sts.
Row 6: Ch 1, sc across, turn.
Rows 7–8: Rep rows 3–4.
Rows 9–10: Rep rows 5–6.
Rows 11–118: Rep rows 7–10, 27 times. Fasten off.

SPIRALS

Note: Chain loosely and work under top loop only of each chain.
Both Ends
(RS) Attach yarn with sl st on corner of one end, sc in next st, ch 15, 3 sc in second ch from hook, 3 sc in each ch to end (42 sc); sc in next 3 sts, ch 20, 3 sc in second ch from hook, 3 sc in each ch to end (57 sc); sc in next 3 sts, ch 25, 3 sc in second ch from hook, 3 sc in each ch to end (72 sc); sc in next 3 sts, ch 20, 3 sc in second ch from hook, 3 sc in each ch to end (42 sc); sc in next 3 sts, ch 15, 3 sc in second ch from hook, 3 sc in each ch to end (42 sc), sl st in last st. Fasten off.

Model made with Brown Sheep Lamb's Pride Super Wash (wool), #SW16 Sea Foam.

Tubular Treasure One

One long, continuous tube of triple crochets forms the foundation for surface embellishment with single crochets.

Finished size approx. 3" x 65" without spirals

materials

Sport weight yarn (168 yds./2.5 oz.), 2 skeins periwinkle (A), 1 skein white (B)
Size H/6 (4mm) crochet hook
Stitch marker
Tapestry needle

gauge

8 tr = 2"
1 row tr = 1.25"

instructions

Note: After rnd 1 work in back lps only and do not join rnds. Place marker at beg of each rnd and move up at end of each rnd.

FOUNDATION TUBE

Rnd 1: With A, ch 25, sc in second ch from hook and each ch, sl st in back lp of first sc — 24 sts.
Rnd 2: Ch 1, sc in first sc, sc in next 7 sts, hdc in next 8 sts, dc in next 8 sts, move up marker.
Rnd 3: Ch 4 (counts as tr and first st), tr in next 23 sts. Work rnds of tr for 61" or to desired length.
Next rnd: Dc in next 8 sts, hdc in next 8 sts, sc in next 8 sts.
Last rnd: Sc in each st around, sl st to beg st. Fasten off.

SURFACE EMBELLISHMENT

With B, join in first free lp with a sc at one end of tube and sc in each free lp to other end of tube. Fasten off.

SPIRALS

Note: Work in top lps only.
First spiral (WS): Join with sl st in any st, ch 24, 3 sc in second ch and each ch to end, sl st in same st. Fasten off.
Second spiral: Skip 7 sts, join with sl st in next st, ch 30, 3 sc in second ch and each ch to end, sl st in same st. Fasten off.
Third spiral: Skip 7 sts, join with sl st in next st, ch 36, 3 sc in second ch and each ch to end, sl st in same st. Fasten off.

Model made with Lion Brand Micro Spun (acrylic), #144 Lilac (A), #100 Lily White (B).

It Takes 13 Hooks!

Yes, you read it correctly — get out your entire hook stash for this one!

Finished size approx. 3"–7" x 75" without tassels

materials

Worsted weight yarn (179 yds. / 2 oz.), 2 skeins purple multicolor

13 sizes crochet hooks: B, C, D, E, F, G, H, I, J, K, L, M, N

Tapestry needle

gauge

With B hook: 14 Esc = 3"

6 rows = 1.5"

special stitch

Extended single crochet (Esc): Insert hook, yo and pull lp through, yo and pull through 1 lp, yo and pull through remaining two lps.

instructions

Row 1: With B hook, ch 15, Esc in second ch from hook and each ch across, turn — 14 sts.

Row 2: Ch 1, Esc in each st across, turn.

Rows 3–6: Ch 1, rep row 2, change to C hook, turn.

Rows 7–12: With C hook rep row 2, change to D hook, turn.

Rows 13–18: With D hook rep row 2, change to E hook, turn.

Rows 19–24: With E hook rep row 2, change to F hook, turn.

Rows 25–30: With F hook rep row 2, change to G hook, turn.

Rows 31–36: With G hook rep row 2, change to H hook, turn.

Rows 37–42: With H hook rep row 2, change to I hook, turn.

Rows 43–48: With I hook rep row 2, change to J hook, turn.

Rows 49–54: With J hook rep row 2, change to K hook, turn.

Rows 55–60: With K hook rep row 2, change to L hook, turn.

Rows 61–66: With L hook rep row 2, change to M hook, turn.

Rows 67–72: With M hook rep row 2 change to N hook, turn.

Rows 73–78: With N hook, rep row 2.

Rows 79–156: Beg with N and ending with B, rep rows 1–78 in reverse. Fasten off.

TASSELS

Refer to directions on page 3.

Model made with Lion Brand Imagine (acrylic / mohair), #338 Purple Haze.

Black And White Checkerboard

Ribbon yarn and lamé thread held together as one combine to make an interesting checkerboard.

Finished size approx. 4" x 52" without fringe

materials

Worsted weight yarn, (110 yds./1.75 oz.), 1 hank each off-white (A), black (B)
Metallic thread, (75 yds./.67 oz.), 1 spool each black (A), pearl (B)
Size K/10.5 (6.5mm) crochet hook
Tapestry needle

gauge

12 dc = 4"
6 rows = 4"

notes

In pattern, A = off-white worsted and black metallic thread held together as one. B = black worsted and pearl metallic thread held together as one. Always drop unused yarn to back side of work.

instructions

Foundation row: With A, ch 6, drop A, pull through B (counts as seventh ch), ch 7, turn — 14 ch.
Row 1 (RS): Dc in fourth st from hook and next 4 sts, dc in next st until 2 lps are left on hook, drop B to back side, pick up A and complete st, dc in next 6 sts, turn — 12 sts.
Row 2: Ch 2 (counts as dc and first st), dc in next 4 sts, dc in next st until 2 lps are left on hook, drop A, pick up B and complete st, dc in next 6 sts, turn.
Row 3: Ch 2, dc in next 4 sts, dc in next st until 2 lps are left on hook, drop B, pick up A and complete st, dc in next 6 sts, turn.
Rows 4–15: Rep rows 2–3. At the end of row 15, cut A (leaving a 6" tail). Cut B in middle of scarf (leaving a 6" tail).
Rows 16–30: Reverse colors, rep rows 1-15, counting ch 2 as dc and first st on row 16.
Rows 31–45: Reverse colors, rep rows 16–30.
Rows 46–60: Reverse colors, rep rows 16–30.
Rows 61–75: Reverse colors, rep rows 16–30.

FRINGE

Use 18 each of black and off-white ribbon. On RS, evenly space 3 black fringes on each white end, and 3 white fringes on each black end. Refer to instructions on page 3.

Model made with Berroco Zen (cotton/nylon ribbon), #8201 Off-White (A), #8253 Black (B); Lion Brand Lamé (polyester/rayon), Black (A), Pearl (B).

Yarn Manufacturers

Berroco Yarns
Elmdale Rd.
P.O. Box 367
Uxbridge, MA 01569
(508) 278-2527
www.berroco.com

Brown Sheep Company
100662 Country Rd. 16
Mitchell, NE 69357
(800) 826-9136
FAX (308) 645-2198
www.brownsheep.com

Bryson Distributing
4065 W. 11th Ave. #39
Eugene, OR 97402
(800) 544-8992
www.brysonknits.com

Classic Elite Yarns, Inc.
300-A Jackson St.
Lowell, MA 01852
(978) 453-2837
www.classiceliteyarns.com

JCA / Artful Yarns
35 Scales Ln.
Townsend MA 01469
(978) 597-8794

Lion Brand Yarns
34 W. 15th St.
New York, NY 10001
(212) 243-8995
FAX (212) 627-8154
www.lionbrand.com

Red Heart / J & P Coats
Consumer Services
P.O. Box 12229
Greenville, SC 29612
(800) 648-1479
www.coatsandclark.com

Trendsetter Yarns
16745 Saticoy St., Suite 101
Van Nuys, CA 91406
(800) 780-5497
FAX (818) 780-5498
www.trendsetteryarn.com

KOOLER DESIGN STUDIO BOOKS
Produced By:
Kooler Design Studio • 399 Taylor Blvd., Ste. 104, Pleasant Hill, CA 94523
kds@koolerdesign.com
Creative Director, Donna Kooler • Editor-in-Chief, Judy Swager
Technical Editor, Marsha Hinkson • Book Design, Nancy Wong Spindler
Photographer, Dianne Woods • Photo Stylist, Basha Kooler Hanner
Models: Melinda Snyder, Ravi Tanner, Courtney Thompson

Published by:
LEISURE ARTS
the art of everyday living

5701 Ranch Drive, Little Rock, AR 72223
www.leisurearts.com
PRINTED WITH SOYINK
Made in U.S.A.